The Complete
Typing Business
Guide

Everything You Need To Know To
Start and Successfully Operate
a Home Typing Business

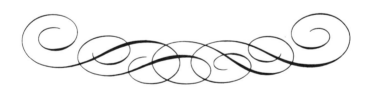

Frank Chisenhall

SuperText Publishing
Honolulu, HI

The Complete TYPING BUSINESS Guide.
Copyright © 1990 by Frank Chisenhall.
Library of Congress Catalog #: 89-63764
Printed and bound in the United States
of America. All rights reserved. No part
of this book may be reproduced in any
form or by any electronic or mechanical
means, including information storage and
retrieval systems, without permission in
writing from the publisher, except by a
reviewer, who may quote brief passages
in a review. Published by SuperText
Publishing, 213-A 4th Street, Honolulu,
HI 96818-4937.

Publisher's
Cataloging in Publication Data

Chisenhall, Frank E.
  The Complete TYPING BUSINESS Guide
Bibliography:p. Includes index.

  1. Typing Business - Home Business.
  2. Secretarial - Home Business.
  3. Typing - Service Industries.
I. Chisenhall, Frank E., 1949-
II. Title.

HF5547. 5. C54   1990   651. 3. 741   89-63764

ISBN   0-9625133-3-4

CONTENTS

The
Home Typing Business

GOOD, FAST MONEY FOR A NEEDED SKILL

A home typing business is one of the most lucrative types of businesses you can start out of your home and can cost almost nothing to get into. Money can be made immediately. The biggest problem most home typists face is not how to get enough business, but how to prevent obligating themselves to type more than they can handle!

There are scores of home typists who make $2,000 or more per month. Many of them started their business as a part time venture while holding down a full time job.

The available number of prospects are staggering. If a person were able to contact all and get them as clients, they would have so many possibilities for typing that they could not handle more than a fraction of the work load.

Chapter One/The Home Typing Business

If the demand is so great, why are more people not into the home typing business? Most people who think about starting a home typing service do not know how to begin. There has been little guidance in this area, and books on the subject are either out of print and therefore hard to find or are 8 to 10 years old and not current.

Those who try to start a business -- whether typing or a different venture -- without knowledge of how, what, where, when, and why usually fail. To do a professional job that people are willing to pay for, to find people who will pay for it, to know all you need to know to start a business and be successful requires knowledge.

In this book, everything you need to know to start and operate a successful home typing business is presented in a clear easy-to-understand text that will have you making money in a matter of days!

Typing clients come from a broad cross-section of people; businesses, individuals, older as well as younger people, and both men and women. The possibilities are limitless.

As a home typist, you possess a skill that is in higher demand today than ever before. Most skilled typists

Chapter One/The Home Typing Business

work for half of what they could get if
they had a typing business of their
own. Conversely, most employers pay
more for secretary and typist employees
than they would if they used the
services of an outside typing agency.

Although an employer pays a secretary
or typist employee less salary than he
or she would pay for your services, the
employer has other employee expenses
that they would not have if they con-
tracted for their typing needs.

The employer has furniture and office
equipment expenses, rent, matching
funds for employee Social Security
payments or some other retirement plan,
vacation pay, costs associated with
absenteeism, medical insurance plans,
and accounting and payroll expenses.

When all these costs are added up, the
employer pays more for an employee than
they would pay you. This fact works to
your advantage and this book tells you
how to turn such information into money
making advertising.

Some small businesses, particularly
those just starting out, cannot afford
to hire secretaries. They are prime
targets for your business advertising.
Getting them as clients is almost as
easy as falling off your typing stool.

However, if they do not know your services exist, their business won't be yours. That's where advertising can pay tremendous dividends. This book will tell you how to get the word out and take in the profits that are waiting for you.

Students and educators need your services for term papers, reports, and theses. People who are looking for or are changing jobs need resume's typed. Writers or authors are looking for typists to put their books, essays, articles, or short stories into printed pages.

Organizations, clubs, and churches need letters/reports/flyers and newsletters typed. Businesses and individuals need many of the above as well as taxes typed. The list can go on. You have the skill to satisfy their needs at a price that will give you a handsome income.

Follow the guidance given in this book and your typing business can be more successful than you imagined, all from the comfort and convenience of your home.

A home typing business will not make you a millionaire. Such claims found in thousands of classified ads are pure "bunk." A typing business will however, give you a steady, reliable income for as long as you want to stay in the business.

To be able to earn good money working for yourself is a great feeling. Being your own boss, calling all the shots, and making money through your own efforts are very rewarding. The effect is hard to equate to any other emotion.

After reading this book, you can put into practice the guidance and be very successful. With effort and a can-do attitude, you can generate far more income than you could get working as a secretary or typist for an employer.

The world is yours; clients are out there eager to give you their business.

If you doubt you
can accomplish
something, then you
can't accomplish
it. You have to
have confidence in
your ability, and
then be tough
enough to follow
through.

— ROSALYNN CARTER

CHAPTER TWO

Getting Started

PERSONAL ATTRIBUTES

The first and most important of anything, whether it is writing, exercis-
ing or beginning a business, is getting
started.   Getting started in the home
typing business is not hard or expensive, but there are a couple of personal attributes the prospective business person must possess.

You must have the ability to type well
if you are going to be the typist.
There is a difference between having an
ability to type and the "two-finger"
typist. Although there are a few "two-
finger" typists who can type as fast as
a typist who uses all fingers, most
type quite slow. Brush up on your
typing skills and you will be well
prepared for your new business.

Further, you must have a strong desire to make your business succeed and faith in your abilities to carry out your wants. Your first hurdle was the purchase of this book. You can read, study the information, and put the knowledge to work in establishing and running a successful home typing business.

This may seem a strange thing to say, but people acquire specialized knowledge that they never use. The real estate profession is a good example. Of the thousands upon thousands of people who go to school and obtain a real estate license, over ninety-five percent never sell real estate! A terrible waste, considering the monetary aspect as well as personal time spent in the training and studying.

EQUIPMENT AND SUPPLIES

There are only a few items of equipment and supplies that you need to start your business.

A good typewriter or word processor is your primary equipment and will be your biggest investment. If you currently have neither, a word processor would be the best investment. Word processors or a word processing software program for a personal computer costs little more than a good typewriter (about $800

on the low end of available systems)
and offers a multitude of attributes
not found in most typewriters.

If you're not sure how to choose a
word processing system, one of the
best books on the market is Word
Processors and Information Processing, by Dan Poynter. Contact Para
Publishing, P. O. Box 4232, Santa
Barbara, CA 93103, for ordering
information.

If you don't want to purchase new equipment, used equipment can be bought from
office equipment companies or from an
individual. The classified ads of most
newspapers have several listings of
people selling typewriters, word processors, or computers. The equipment is
always used, but the price can be as
much as fifty percent below the price
of a new one and about thirty percent
below the cost of a used one from an
office equipment firm.

If you decide to purchase from a classified ad, call and get some information
first.

Find out the make, model, and year of
the equipment. Ask how long the person
has had the equipment and why they are
selling it. After you get this information, call an office equipment firm and
find out how much they would sell the

same equipment for. This is a good way to get an initial feel for whether the equipment price is right.

Always examine the equipment before you buy it. Here are some helpful hints:

1. Typewriters.

A. Visually check the keys to ensure they are not excessively worn or loose.

B. Check the platen (the roller of a typewriter) to ensure it is still semisoft, not dried out, pitted or otherwise damaged.

C. Place a sheet of typing paper into the machine and use the carriage return to advance the paper. The action should advance the paper evenly.

D. While you have the paper in the typewriter, type each row of letters or numbers at least three times. If the characters print up or below each other rather than level, don't print at all, or print light for some and dark for others, don't purchase the equipment. It would be too expensive to repair.

2. Word Processors.

A. Turn the equipment on and try it out. If the disk drive "thumps" loudly or continually, the head is out of alignment and will cost a considerable amount to repair. Some software thumps by design, but not as a rule. You take a chance on big repair bills by buying disk drives that thump.

B. Ensure the word processor has a spell-check capability, underline, right justify, and copy and move functions, as a minimum. You also must have the word processing manual (software documentation) or you will not be able to use the attributes of the word processor. Ensure the system has at least 64,000 bytes of RAM (random access memory). This equates to about 20-25 pages of type.

C. Check the printer to guarantee it works properly and prints letter-quality. The print head should have a minimum 16 dots (pins), in-line vertical. A print head with 24 dots is best. Your clients need their documents letter quality. The print speed should be at least 25 CPS (characters per second).

D. Check the type of printer ribbon used. If the printer uses a carbon ribbon, it is a one-pass ribbon. While the type looks much better than the conventional cloth ribbon, a carbon ribbon is expensive and can only be used once. This in itself is not a reason for not buying the word processor, but it is information you need to be aware of.

3. Computers.

Since you are purchasing the computer only if a word processing system is included, check the same features and other hints provided previously for word processors.

If you are not sure you want to invest in a typewriter or word processing system because of the cost, you can rent the equipment at a reasonable rate. Borrowing the equipment from a relative is also an option.

If you already have a word processing system or a typewriter, you are dollars ahead on getting started. If you only have a typewriter, don't worry. Don't run out and buy a word processing system because of it.

Many home typing businesses started out with a typewriter and then graduated to a word processor after the business was well established. Also, there are several home typing businesses that started with a typewriter and still use one, and they are quite successful.

The standard typewriter has 10 or 12 pitch type to choose from and will type either Pica (large type) or Elite (somewhat smaller type). Of course, there are IBM brand typewriters that have typing elements (IBM balls) that can be changed to give a large variety of type fonts (an assortment of type styles). But the standard 10 or 12 pitch, Pica or Elite typewriter will be adequate for most of your typing jobs.

After you have your equipment lined up, you will need to ensure you have enough supplies on hand. Typing paper will be your most-used and frequently-purchased supply. Here, your goal is to maintain low cost and still provide a quality product. The most common good quality, low-cost typing paper is twenty pound, twenty-five percent cotton fiber.

(NOTE: Don't use erasable bond paper unless a client specifically asks for it. This type of paper is simple to erase on, but smudges easily and can ruin a very good typing job).

To start out, you have no need to pur- chase large amounts of paper. One or two packages (or reams, which are usu- ally cheaper) will be enough and will help keep your start-up costs low.

Check several stores to get the best bargain. It is not bad advice to stick with one supplier when you have a good one, but keep checking other sources. Many times regular customers are taken for granted and better services are provided to new customers. If this happens to you, do not feel obligated to stay with one supplier. Their business is important, but yours is too.

Besides paper, you will also need an adequate supply of the following:

1.   Carbon paper (if you are using a typewriter or if a customer asks for carbons even though you store on diskettes when using a word processing system).

2.   An accordion file for keeping records and correspondence.

3.   Paper clips, stapler and staples.

4.   A good supply of various denominations of postage stamps.

5.   9" X 12" envelopes (and cardboard inserts to keep the pages from being folded).

6.   Typewriter or printer ribbons (and correction ribbons if your typewriter has that feature).

7.   Scotch brand tape.

8.   Assorted rubber bands.

9.   Correction fluid (if your typewriter does not   have   a   correction
feature).

10.   A record ledger for   your   business.

11.   A record ledger or address   book
to   keep   client   data (3" X 5"   cards
will also work).

12.   A good dictionary.

Many   other supplies such as   letterhead
stationery   are not listed because   they
are   unnecessary start-up expenses.   You
will   want   nice letterhead   stationery,
business   envelopes,   a   work   station,
postage   scale, desk lamp, and a   myriad
of   other things after your business   is
a   going concern.   But they are not   the
types   of   expenses   you need   to   worry
about   incurring when you are trying   to
keep your start up costs to a minimum.

Use what talents
you possess; the
woods would be
very silent if no
birds sang there
except those that
sang best.

— HENRY VAN DYKE

The

Shoestring Operation

A TYPING BUSINESS AT MINIMUM COST

FREE ADVERTISING

When you first begin your typing business, you do not have to invest large amounts of money to make money. If you want to keep your expenses to a minimum <u>do not</u> use paid advertising, buy letterhead stationery, open a business bank account, get a business phone or buy postage scales. These expenses you <u>will have</u> when you decide to project an image of a full service typing business.

This chapter is for those who are not yet interested in a full time business but still want to make money typing at home. This can be done, and free advertising will be discussed first.

Chapter three/The Shoestring Operation

Many times you see advertisements that say this or that is free, and the first thought you have is, "What's the catch?" The only catch in the free advertising discussed here is that it is not "free" in the absolute sense; it will cost you some effort.

It is free in that you are not paying $1.00-6.00 per word to advertise; there is no "up-front" money outlay to place a burden on your business start-up costs.

The best free advertising is use of BULLETIN BOARDS. These are common everywhere, and have probably sold more goods and services than all the combined salespeople you could compare them with. Bulletin boards are one of the most powerful, free advertising medias you will ever use.

Everyone reads bulletin boards, whether out of curiosity, boredom, or looking for bargains. And your advertising is not "spent" as it is in paid newspaper or magazine advertising; it stays on the bulletin board until you decide to remove it.

The bulletin boards you want to target are many. Remember though, that before posting on most bulletin boards, you will need to get approval beforehand. No charge, just approval.

Your advertisement will either be stamped or initialed by the approving authority, and dated. Now, here is a list of the bulletin boards you want to target.

JUNIOR HIGH, HIGH SCHOOL, COLLEGES, AND UNIVERSITIES.

These are your best targets for bulletin board advertising. Students are always tasked to write and type documents of some form or another and most of the students are not typists. In fact, even those who can type often have other things they would rather be doing than typing and will gladly pay someone to perform this chore.

When typing for students, maintain the same professional quality that you do for anyone else. Not only will it help secure good grades for the student (provided, of course, that the content meets the instructor's requirements), but will also result in repeat business and word-of-mouth referrals. You might want to offer a first time introductory offer --such as ten percent discount -- or free delivery within a 5-mile radius (for jobs $25.00 and up).

You can encourage quicker customer response if your discounts have a time limit -- say for the next 30 days -- that they are in effect.

23

A sample ad might read something like
this:

ARE THE BEST PARTIES, MOVIES, TRIPS OR
EVENTS OF THE CENTURY INTERFERING WITH
YOUR NEED TO TYPE A REPORT OR PAPER?
ENJOY YOURSELF AND LET ME HELP YOU!
I'LL TYPE THE PAPERS FOR YOU; NEAT,
PROFESSIONAL, AND IN WHATEVER FORMAT
YOU SPECIFY. MY RATES ARE VERY
REASONABLE AND ARE LISTED BELOW:

$1.50 PER DOUBLE-SPACED PAGE (WITHOUT
FOOTNOTES; $2.50 WITH FOOTNOTES).

$5.00 MINIMUM.

1 1/4" TO 1 1/2" ALL AROUND MARGINS.

20 LB, 25% COTTON BOND.

24 HOUR TURN AROUND TIME!

(IF YOUR DOCUMENT IS SUBMITTED BEFORE
_____, I'LL GIVE YOU A 10%
DISCOUNT! NOTE:10% Discount does not
apply to minimum charges.) ALL
MAILINGS POSTPAID! CONTACT: XXX
Typing Service, Address, Phone
number.

Ads are typed neatly on 5" X 8" cards
and placed in the most prominent
position (eye level, middle of the

board), if possible. Outlining the border of the card in RED also helps to attract the eye when scanning.

Another idea to consider is "tabbing" the bottom of your index card (cutting several strips upward from the bottom) and putting your phone number on the tab.

This is useful for students who do not have a pen or pencil available to write down your address or phone number; they can just tear off the "tab" and keep it with them until they have an opportunity to call you.

Be sure and write "TYPING" on the back side of the tab so it will identify what the phone number is for. Tabbing has another benefit too; when you check and see several tabs missing it will let you know that people are considering your services.

It also tells other prospective clients that your business services are being used by their peers (some bulletin board advertisers tear off a tab or two themselves to create this impression!)

Keep close account of your bulletin board ads and do not allow them to become obsolete. If your ten percent discount ended March 31, have a new 5" X 8" card posted April 1.

Slant your advertising on the cards to take advantage of current youth or community interests. If the big drawing card for youth is professional football in the city, then you could start your ad with:

"THE PROFESSIONAL FOOTBALL SEASON IS HERE AND YOU CAN'T ATTEND BECAUSE YOU HAVE A RESEARCH OR TERM PAPER YOU HAVE TO TYPE?... "

Locations where bulletin boards can usually be found in junior high and high schools are:

(1) outside of classroom entrances, (2) main hallways, (3) outside the Principal's office, (4) in the school library, (5) in the Gym, (6) in the cafeteria, and (7) Home Ec classes. For colleges, you can also find bulletin boards in dormitories, sorority and fraternity houses, etc. They are everywhere! All it costs you is the 5" X 8" card and your typing of the ad.

Besides schools and universities, bulletin boards are many other places:

The Post Office, city recreation centers, churches, laundromats, and at your and/or your spouse's work place.

Many PUBLIC and PRIVATE clubs usually

have bulletin boards too. Check them all out. The more advertising you do, the more exposure you get to potential clients!

Keep a record of all your bulletin board advertising and any "specials" you have offered. Review often and update as necessary.

To advertise in all the places just mentioned will require quite a few 5" X 8" cards. To type cards for thirty to fifty bulletin boards would be too time-consuming. There is a better way to do it.

For example, decide how many cards you need for junior high and high schools. Type up two index cards (on the side without lines) and give the message you want. Draw your tab lines on each card (where you want to cut) and write or type your phone number on each tab.

Place the cards on an 8 1/2" X 11" sheet of paper and tape them down with your Scotch brand tape. Take the pasted up sheet to your local copy center and ask them to run the number of copies you need (remember you will get two cards per sheet) on white "book cover" stock. You now have all your cards. With cover stock at ten to fifteen cents a sheet, you have saved a lot of time and money.

27

Chapter three/The Shoestring Operation

Do the same procedure for all the other bulletin boards you want to use. After printing, just cut apart and cut your tab lines.

When your clients pay with a check or money order, have it made out in your name rather than your business name. You can then deposit the money in your personal bank account without the expense of opening a business checking account.

Business checking accounts usually charge a monthly service fee (about three dollars), a fee for each check deposited or written (fifteen cents), a fee for any customer checks that are returned (about two dollars), and sometimes other fees. Business checking accounts are important and necessary, however, if you are establishing a full time typing business that requires a professional image.

You must keep accurate records regard-less of whether you deposit money to your personal account or to a business checking account. Local, state and federal taxes must be paid on your net business profits.

TERM PAPERS, RESEARCH PAPERS, BOOK REPORTS.

You may receive these from high school

28

and college students or instructors who are pursuing an advanced degree while holding teaching jobs. Formats vary depending on instructors, so always ask for the format they want. When foot- noting is a part of the document, your charge for each page should be adjusted upward because of the difficulty. How to set charges for your work will be in a later chapter.

TAX RETURNS.

These will be from individuals and are mostly "fill in the blank" type of forms. Attachments to forms require reference to the form block you are continuing and do not present format problems.

EMPLOYMENT APPLICATIONS.

These are normally of a "fill in the blank" nature and are simple. Again, continuation information is typed on plain bond and the block that is being continued is referenced. For example, if you were typing in additional pre- vious employment information for block #6, you would type on the continuation sheet:

Block #6, Previous Employment Information (continued).

Type in the added information. Skip two

lines between separate entries.

The above categories are the major Kinds of documents you will receive to type when using bulletin board advertising. They are not all inclusive.

As your business professionalism is spread "word-of-mouth" by your satisfied clients, you will get more than enough typing to provide you with a steady, well-earned income.

CHAPTER FOUR

Structure, Name,

Taxes and License

YOUR BUSINESS STRUCTURE

When you establish your typing business, you will need to decide what type
of business operation you want. There
are three primary types:

    Sole proprietorship
    Partnership
    Corporation

Most home-operated businesses begin as
a sole proprietorship. It is the
easiest and cheapest form of business
to establish.

A sole proprietorship is a one-owner
business. No special license is required to establish and conduct business. However, most states require the
name and activity of your business to
be registered with the state.

The sole proprietorship has several advantages:

Profits and losses of the business are reported on the owner's personal income tax return for both State and Federal returns.

Business decisions can be made quickly because there are no other owners whose approval is needed.

It is easy to get started. Open the doors and begin!

You have maximum authority and complete freedom of action concerning the business.

There are some disadvantages of a sole proprietorship also:

As the owner, you have unlimited liability for mistakes or damages to others that result from the conduct of your business.

If the owner dies, the sole proprietorship is dissolved.

The growth of the sole proprietorship is limited to the initiatives of the owner.

A partnership is a business owned and

operated by two or more persons. An agreement is drawn up defining the responsibilities of each partner. There are advantages and disadvantages of a partnership arrangement. Advantages are:

More than one person is involved in solving business problems and ideas are better.

The financing of the business is less trouble because the expenses are spread among the owners.

Business losses are shared among the owners.

There are some disadvantages too:

All partners are liable for the acts and debts of all the other partners.

Disagreements among partners as to how the business should be conducted.

Hard to get a bad partner out of the business unless specifically provided for in the partnership agreement.

The third and final major business type that will be discussed is the corporation. A corporation is a legal entity that is separate from the sole proprietorship and partnership. A corporation must have a board of directors and elected officers of the corporation for running day-to-day operations. All assets are owned by the corporation, not individuals.

Corporations have advantages and disadvantages. Some of the advantages are:

Liability for operation of the business is limited to the assets of the business, not the assets of the shareholders.

Death of a shareholder does not affect the legality of the corporation.

Shares that represent ownership can be transferred to others.

Corporations can usually raise additional capital needs easier than a sole proprietorship or a partnership.

Tax deductions and general tax treatment can be better for corporations than for individuals.

The disadvantages are:

Establishing corporations is costly.

The state and federal laws governing corporations require considerable paperwork that must be submitted. Activities of corporations are watched closely by both state and federal organizations.

Profits given to shareholders are taxed twice. The corporation pays tax on the profits and the shareholders pay tax on the distributed profits.

NAME YOUR BUSINESS

When you begin your typing business, you will need a name for it. You can use your own name or you can make up one. If you are going to advertise in the local telephone Yellow Pages, you should keep the alphabet in mind when choosing your business name.

Suppose you do not use your own name and decide to make up one. Can you choose just any name? There are some restrictions.

You cannot use a name that is already a trade name or trademark. Everyone knows that IBM, Sony, etc. are trademark names. What about those names that are not so well known?

You can use a name that is not trademarked, but you must be careful. If the name belongs to a firm that has conducted business under that name frequently before the public then that business has ownership rights to use that name.

How should you choose a name? First,
sit and make a list of names you want
to consider. They should reflect trust
and strength, not be perceived as harm-
ful to your business (i. e. , Typo Typing
Service or Temporary Typing) and not be
too long. Length affects advertising
costs!

After you have made your list -- maybe
forty to fifty possibles -- check it
against the telephone Yellow Pages
under "Secretarial Services", "Typists"
or "Printing Services. " For every name
on your list that is already being
used, cross it out.

When you finish with the Yellow Pages,
go to the White Pages. Match your remaining names and cross out those
already being used. The names you have
left are your candidates.

This does not ensure you have not used
a name someone elsewhere in the state
is using. There are other sources you
can check if you want to be reasonably
sure no one else is using the name you
choose.

You can check with your state Department of Taxation to determine if a
general excise license was issued under
the trade name. The United States
Patent Office publishes the <u>Official
Gazette of the U. S. Patent Office,</u>

and it can usually be found in the government documents section of your local library. Private companies which conduct trade name, trademark and service mark searches are a good source. Trade bureaus and associations as well as service firms that deal in the same type of business you do round out the recommended sources to check.

Some states require you to register your trade name while others do not. Check with your state Department of Commerce and Consumer Affairs to be sure. If you do register with your state they will usually check to make sure no one else has a "substantially identical" registration.

TAXES

After you have chosen your business name and checked about registration, contact your state Department of Taxation. Many states will require you to obtain a general excise tax license and pay a small fee (one to five dollars).

You will be required to pay an excise tax on the GROSS sales or earnings of your business and may also be required to collect state sales tax on services you provide to residents of your state. These taxes are separate from state income taxes. State income taxes can be reduced when you subtract your business expenses. Ask for the Small Business Tax Guide from your state tax office.

You are required to pay federal taxes on your net income. The IRS can provide you with the proper tax guides for small businesses to ensure you file properly and pay only your legal share of taxes.

Although federal taxes and the laws applying to them are considered complex, the IRS publishes several guides that explain the many facets of paying taxes. After reading and studying these publications and forms, anyone can file their own taxes. If you decide to have a tax expert prepare yours, order and read these publications and forms to understand exactly what tax breaks and liabilities you have. It never hurts to keep yourself informed.

For your home typing business, order the following FREE publications and forms. You can order one copy of each publication and two copies of each form. Allow two weeks processing time after the IRS receives your order.

PUBLICATIONS:

#1   Your Rights As A Taxpayer
#17   Your Federal Income Tax (Be
      sure and get this one!)

#505   Tax Withholding and Estimated
       Tax
#525   Taxable and Nontaxable Income
#529   Miscellaneous Deductions
#534   Depreciation
#535   Business Expenses
#536   Net Operating Losses
#545   Interest Expense
#572   General Business Credit
#587   Business Use of Your Home
#596   Earned Income Credit
#917   Business Use of a Car
#910   A complete list of all avail-
       able IRS publications with
       descriptions.

FORMS:

Form 1040   U. S. Individual Income Tax
            Return
Schedule A   Itemized Deductions
Schedule B   Interest Income More Than
             $400
Schedule C   Profit or Loss From
             Business
Schedule E   Supplemental Income
             Schedule
Schedule SE Social Security Self-
             Employment Tax
1040-ES   Estimated Tax For
          Individuals
Form 4562   Depreciation and
            Amortization

Obtain the publications and forms listed using the addresses below.

STATE: Alaska, Arizona, California, Colorado, Hawaii, Idaho, Montana, Nevada, New Mexico, Oregon, Utah, Washington, Wyoming.
ADDRESS: Forms Distribution Center, Rancho Cordova, CA 95743-0001.

STATE: Alabama, Arkansas, Illinois, Indiana, Iowa, Kansas, Kentucky, Louisiana, Michigan, Minnesota, Mississippi, Missouri, Nebraska, North Dakota, Ohio, Oklahoma, South Dakota, Tennessee, Texas, Wisconsin.
ADDRESS: Forms Distribution Center, P. O. Box 9903, Bloomington, IL 61799.

STATE: Connecticut, Delaware, District of Columbia, Florida, Georgia, Maine, Maryland, Massachusetts, New Hampshire, New Jersey, New York, North Carolina, Pennsylvania, Rhode Island, South Carolina, Vermont, Virginia, West Virginia.
ADDRESS: Forms Distribution Center, p. o. Box 25866, Richmond, VA 23289.

Taxes are based on sales so keep good records of income and expenses. Be thorough in recording expenses and keeping receipts. These are most important when you determine state and federal income tax liability!

LICENSE

The last item, licenses, requires very little to say. For most home-based service businesses, a business license is not required. Keep in mind that registering a business and getting a business license are two different things. However, each state has its own laws, so be sure to check with your local authorities to get the particulars for your state.

Dare to be wise;
begin!He who
postpones the
hour of living
rightly is like
the rustic who
waits for the
river to run out
before he
crosses.

— HORACE

Expanding

Your Business

ESTABLISHING AN IMAGE

When you have made the decision to have your business grow beyond the shoe-string operation and become a full time typing concern, you need to take action to establish your professional image.

You want to have letterhead stationery, envelopes and business cards. These products help depict your business as a professional, established concern that is permanent and trustworthy.

Your local copy center/print shop can provide these items. Review the different fonts and type styles and choose one appropriate for your business.

Chapter Five/Expanding Your Business

Stationery, envelopes and business cards are cheaper when ordered in quantity. A quantity of 500 sheets of letterhead, 500 envelopes and 200 business cards should be the maximum first order you place.

Typesetting of these items will cost you in the range of $30 to $50. The stationery, envelopes and business cards will total about $80 to $100 for the quantities recommended. Shop around for the best price before you place your order.

After you start using these items, the types of products you will receive for typing will be expanded. These items will be used in your promotion and advertising efforts explained in later chapters and will open the doors to additional typing clients. The following paragraphs discuss typing products you will receive.

WHAT YOU WILL TYPE

MANUSCRIPTS.

These will be received from writers (authors) and will consist of short stories, articles, plays, books, query letters and outlines. In most cases, you will receive the needed format from your client. A standard manuscript format is included in the appendix of this book for your use if your client doesn't give you the format they want.

In all cases, the typing will be double-spaced and NOT on erasable bond paper.

Typing for writers is one of the best client/business relationships you can get because of the repeat business. For example, initial typing is normally a draft. The draft is then edited and polished by the writer and returned for another typing.

When you give timely, professional service, other writing submissions will follow. Because the writer's income and livelihood are directly proportional to the amount of work they produce and sell, you could keep busy servicing these type of accounts.

RESUMES.

This is a product that you may receive often. With the mobile society we have, people are constantly submitting resumes for new and better jobs. A standard resume format is also in the appendix.

TERM PAPERS, RESEARCH PAPERS, BOOK REPORTS.

These were discussed in chapter three.

You may receive these from high school and college students or instructors who are pursuing an advanced degree while holding teaching jobs. Formats vary depending on instructors, so always ask for the format they want. When footnoting is a part of the document, your charge for each page should be adjusted upward because of the difficulty. How to set charges for your work will be in a later chapter.

LETTERS (BUSINESS, PERSONAL, SALES).

These are usually submitted with formats. If they are not, ask for one because the types of formats are many and varied. You could end up typing the same document twice -- one time for nothing!

Most businesses will provide you with letterhead paper for their typing. For personal letters, twenty pound bond paper is enough.

FINANCIAL REPORTS.

These you may get from small businesses and nonprofit organizations. They are usually simple balance sheet or summary reports. They will be submitted in the format your client wants. If not, ask.

TAX RETURNS.

These and employment applications were also discussed in chapter three. Submissions will probably be from small businesses and individuals and are "fill in the blank" type of forms. Attachments to forms only require reference to the form block you are continuing and do not present format problems.

EMPLOYMENT APPLICATIONS.

These are normally of a "fill in the blank" nature and are simple. Again, continuation information is typed on plain bond and the block that is being continued is referenced. For example, if you were typing in additional previous employment information for block #6, you would type on the continuation sheet:

Block #6, Previous Employment
Information (continued).

Type in the added information. Skip two lines between separate entries.

MEDICAL TRANSCRIPTS, INSURANCE FORMS.

These have general formats and present few problems. Additional care must be taken when typing medical papers. The spelling must be verified because of the unique terminology used in this profession and the difference that could be inferred from misspelling.

The above categories are the major kinds of documents you will receive to type. They are not all inclusive.

As emphasized before, when your business professionalism is spread "word-of-mouth" by your satisfied clients, you will get more than enough typing to provide you with a steady, well-earned income.

Speaking of income, it is time to discuss how much you should charge for your work.

CHAPTER SIX

Getting Paid

THE PRICE TO CHARGE

When people submit documents to you for typing, they expect a professional job; no smudges or fingerprints, no wrinkled papers, no typos, no stapled pages, and the document in the right format. Like-wise, when you do a professional job, you expect to get paid the going rate for professional typists.

PER PAGE PRICES

Always get paid "up front" for your jobs! Basic rates range from $1.50 per double-spaced (DS) page on up. The $1.50 per DS page should be for simple typing. When you are typing single-spaced pages or documents with foot-notes and complex formats, you should increase your rates accordingly.

Single-spaced pages should bring at least $3.00 per page and DS pages with footnotes and/or complex formats should bring $3.50-$3.75 per page.

With these rates, you can absorb postage charges. If you type at a lesser rate than these, charge your customer for postage.

Set a minimum charge for your work. At least a $5.00 minimum, even for one page. This will ensure your time and efforts are not used up on one-page jobs and will keep your average hourly income at a respectable level.

Although the foregoing are basic rates, it is always wise to check out what your competition is charging.

Most of the large typing concerns are listed in your phone book Yellow Pages under "Secretarial Services", "Printing Services" or "Typists". You want to be competitive but you do not want to raise your prices drastically if you find that your competition is charging more than you. Producing a professional product at a lesser charge is something that you can use in your advertising.

Remember that large organizations, un-like your home-based business, must pay overhead costs in addition to salaries and benefits. These reasons drive their pricing policy.

If your rates are higher than your competition, you don't have to lower them. Stress the major advantages of your business, such as timeliness, better quality, and personalized service.

CHARGING AN HOURLY RATE

Several home typing businesses charge an hourly rate rather than a per-page rate. Others charge an hourly rate for businesses that need a steady volume of typing and a per-page rate for individuals or others with sporadic typing needs. The hourly rate should range from twelve to fifteen dollars.

The hourly rate charges can be set up as follows:

1. Minimum charge: one(1) hour ($15.00).

2. Fractions of an hour over the minimum:

   A. 01-10 minutes = $3.50

   B. 11-20 minutes = $6.50

   C. 21-30 minutes = $8.50

   D. 31 minutes plus = a full hour.

When you charge by the hour, document your time for your benefit as well as the benefit of your client. Prepare a record of your time in duplicate; one for your records and one for your customer. A sample time sheet might look like the one on the next page.

A form like this allows your clients to see actual typing time they are paying for and how much time it took to type a particular document.

If you make a typing mistake, you are obligated to correct the problem free of charge. If the mistake was in the document provided by the client, the retyping is at their expense. Anytime a job is returned with a mistake, check and verify you made the mistake before you agree to correct it free of charge.

Some businesses may want to keep your services on-call, paying you a monthly retainer fee. These fees are good income, but you incur an obligation to the client to be available anytime they need you; anytime! If you have another project you are working on, you must put it aside and take care of the client who has you on retainer. Something to keep in mind if you are offered the option of being on retainer.

ABC TYPING SERVICE
P. O. BOX 1222
ANYWHERE, USA

Worksheet
For: Date:

Total
Charges:

Document Name	Start Time	Stop Time	RSN Stop	Time Charge

Reason for stops (RSN Stop):
TEL = Telephone Interruption
BRK = Took a Break
OTH = Other Interruptions
COMP= Document typing completed

When charging an hourly rate, the business client may pay you when they pay their other payroll obligations or when they pay their operating expenses. State in writing what your expectations are. Ensure what you want and what the client thinks you want are the same. It is upsetting to expect to be paid bi-weekly only to find out your client plans to pay monthly!

Additional tips that you should consider are:

1. For typing manuscripts (stories, articles, novels, etc.), you should not charge full price for the title page since it will only have four to six typewritten lines. Thirty to forty cents for the title page and the last page (if it is less than ten type-written lines) would be fair. The author will appreciate it and will give you repeat business.

2. Mail your typing using the special Manuscript Rate. Ask for it at the Post Office when you mail out your completed product. If a customer asks for First Class mail, charge them for it. They will pay the additional charge if they need the document First Class.

3. Don't staple the pages of documents together; use paper clips or leave the pages loose. If the customer wants to

staple it, they will ask for it or
they will do it themselves.

4. Never promise what you cannot de-
liver. When someone brings a document
to you for typing and wants it completed in two hours and you know it will
take three, tell them so. If you lose
the customer that is better than rush-
ing your work, missing the time limit,
and not getting paid at all!

5. Odd hour (late night) or rush jobs
where a project in progress must be
set aside demands higher rates. Set
your policies (24 hours turn around
for small jobs less than twenty pages
and larger jobs on a progressive
scale). If a client wants their document quicker than that, consider a surcharge for the job. If you do not get
the submission during odd hours or do
not have a job in progress, the normal
rate would be fair.

However, if the "rush" job causes a
backlog for you, quote the surcharge
up front to the customer (30-60 cents
per page extra, $6.00 minimum) and re-
mind them of your 24-hour policy. Some
will wait while others will pay the
charge. Few will decline to use your
services because of the surcharge. Be
realistic about your professional time
schedule; your customers will be also.

6. If you are using a typewriter you can control your bottom-of-the-page by marking your page lightly with a pencil at the left margin. After the page is removed from the typewriter the mark can be erased. If using a word processor, set the bottom of the page using the print options within your program. The bottom margin is automatically taken care of.

7. Some clients may ask that their document text be "right-justified," having each line of type end flush with the right margin in a block style. Good word processing systems have this capability. If you are using a typewriter, don't offer this service or accept documents that must be right justified. Doing right justification manually (on a typewriter) is so time consuming that your efforts would result in a loss of profit.

8. Check all documents for spelling errors, typos and punctuation. Most word processing systems have spell-check capabilities and some have punctuation checks, functions that can be performed before you print the document. For long documents, this capability saves time and effort. If you are using a typewriter, check the document while it is still in the typewriter. Read through it slowly to check spelling and punctuation.

After reading the document, read it again BACKWARDS. This is one of the best manual methods known for catching misspelled words, although it is time consuming.

9. Be prompt and courteous to your customers. For businesses, this seems to be a dying virtue. It creates untold frustration for customers when they don't get their completed documents on time or the business treats them like mechanical objects. Complete your work on time and be nice to your clients. This goodwill pays dividends in repeat business and free word-of-mouth advertising.

10. In the typing business, one carbon copy is free and additional copies are five cents each. Copy machine copies should be 12 cents each. If you have a word processor or a computer, offer free disk storage for 30 days. Over that, offer continued storage for a small fee ($1.00 per month per disk).

Speaking of advertising, the next chapter will discuss where you get your clients from and how to write advertising copy that will get you all the business you can handle!

Universal Intelligencer.

Vol. XXIV.

APRIL, 1871.

No. 13.

Always bear in mind that your own resolution to succeed is more important than any one thing.

—ABRAHAM LINCOLN

CHAPTER SEVEN

Promotion

GETTING THE WORD OUT

When you first open for business, you can write news releases for local newspapers and magazines. Your community library will have a list of all local newspapers and magazines with addresses, editor's names, and phone numbers of who to contact.

Your news release should concentrate on the services you provide and benefits of those services for the community. Talk about the need to solve a problem and then give the solution -- your typing services.

News releases do not have to be limited to announcing your business opening. They can also be used to announce rates, changes in rates, changes in your business address, changes in types of material accepted for typing, changes in geographical areas served, changes in your equipment (upgrades), services other than those mentioned above, special rates offered for a limited period of time, etc.

Anything that is of community interest is good for news releases. News releases are free and are accepted better by the paying public than advertising. Advertising is looked upon as self-serving while news is looked at as more truthful. News releases seem to generate as much or more business than straight advertising.

A part time entrepreneur in Virginia who makes homemade knives ran classified ads in local and regional newspapers. The sales generated from classified advertising paid a fair income above the advertising and knife production expenses.

A staff writer from one of the regional newspapers saw the "Knives for Sale" sign in front of the knife maker's home and stopped by to check out the product. The writer was impressed with the quality. He asked some questions, took some pictures, and wrote an article for his newspaper. Knife sales jumped over eight hundred percent within one week! Many buyers drove more than one hundred miles just to purchase the knives.

The news release is sent to the newspaper or magazine editor. Some will
print it as written while others may
reword it. A few may even decide to
write a feature story on your business
and may contact you for an interview.

You can prepare for the phone call or
an interview. Sit and write out a list
of questions you would ask if you knew
nothing about a typing business. Then,
write out the best answers you believe
will fully satisfy the question.

Keep this question and answer list
close to your telephone. Refer to it
often.

The interview could be over the telephone. If you read the questions and
answers often enough, you will be at
ease when interviewed about your business.

Writing a news release is not difficult. The format is basic. Type "NEWS
RELEASE" on your letterhead stationery
(or a plain piece of bond paper that
contains your company name and address
at the top) centered below your address.

About three spaces down, type the date
the news is to be released or type "FOR
IMMEDIATE RELEASE. " This information
is typed flush with the right margin.

Give a contact name (a friend's or yours) and phone number.

Skip two more spaces and give the headline (all caps). The headline should be an attention-getter. Space down two more lines and begin the main part of your release.

Give your priority information first and the less important data last. Editors do not always have enough space to include your total news release and may cut from the end.

Identify the problem and the need to solve it. Give the solution -- your business services. A sample news release is given on the next two pages. Note the format and the content.

Remember the rules to follow and pick out the steps that the sample news release contains.

Type your news release double-spaced on 8 1/2 X 11" paper and maintain margins at 1 1/2" all around. Try to keep the release short; a single page is what you should strive for. Your news release should contain the "-30-" newspaper termination (end) sign.

If your news release is two pages, type "(more)," centered, at the bottom of the first page.

Type Right Services
P. O. Box 112
Jill, TX 77777

NEWS RELEASE

FOR IMMEDIATE RELEASE
Contact: Judy Towers
(807) 555-1212

AFFORDABLE TYPING SERVICES OFFERED TO BUSINESSES AND INDIVIDUALS

Type Right Services is a secretarial
business created to provide professional, timely and affordable typing for
businesses and individuals. Type Right
Services not only supplement the typing
needs of large firms; they enable the
small business and individuals to obtain professionally-typed products
without the expense of hiring a permanent typist or secretary.

Secretaries are expensive. Salaried em-
ployees require payroll and tax record
Keeping, fringe benefits such as
(More)

vacation and sick pay, and pension con-
tributions or matching funds for Social
Security. These expenses are eliminated
when using Type Right Services.

Run by a professional typist, Type
Right Services offers hourly rates for
businesses and per-page rates for individuals. Formats provided by the clients or standard formats offered by
Type Right Services gives that ever
important, professional touch to correspondence or personal writing.

Judy Towers, the owner of Type Right
Services, has over 10 years of professional typing experience. By her estimate, over 10 million words have been
produced through her fingertips. Besides the personal care given to each
client, turn-around time for most documents submitted is 24 hours; hard to
beat by anybody's standards.

For further information on the various
services provided and a complete rate
sheet, call (807) 555-1212, or write to
Type Right Services, P. O. Box 112,
Jill, TX 77777.

-30-

RATE SHEETS. Your rate sheets show your clients what your services cost. Make a rate sheet for businesses (hourly rates) and a rate sheet for per-page rates (individuals). Include a copy of each with your news release.

Always include a copy in any direct mail campaign and when answering a new client query. Make up a rate sheet using the sample provided in Chapter Six.

Keep away from
people who try
to belittle your
ambitions. Small
people always do
that, but the
really great
make you feel
that you, too, can
become great.

— MARK TWAIN

CHAPTER EIGHT

Advertising
Your Business

FREE ADVERTISING

Many times you see advertisements that
say this or that is free, and the first
thought you have is, "What's the catch?"
The only catch in the free advertising
discussed here is that it is not "free"
in the absolute sense; it will cost you
some effort.

It is free in that you are not paying
$1.00-6.00 per word to advertise; there
is no large money outlay to place a burden on your business start-up costs.

In Chapter Three we discussed using bulletin boards as a method of free advertising. Now we will discuss another
method you can use.

INTRODUCTORY LETTERS.

These letters are free advertising. Of course the term "free" is again tainted somewhat, because you do have to pay for postage and the stationery used. But when compared to several dollars per word or line in a newspaper or magazine ad, they are virtually free.

These letters can be sent to school teachers, college professors, church ministers, doctors, lawyers, dentists, other small businesses, and clubs such as Lions, Rotary, DAR, YMCA, YWCA, Scouting organizations, etc.

Your introductory letter should be friendly, state the various types of services that you offer, give a brief statement about your qualifications, emphasize your quality and timeliness, and give a brief list of your rates charged.

Use plain English, stay away from sensa- tional statements and flowery adjec- tives, and do not try "hard ball" pres- sure tactics. Conclude your letter with a brief paragraph something like, "If you have a need for our services, just call or write. We are in business to help you." Always include your phone number and address, of course (this is where letterhead stationery pays off). Chapter Ten has some sample letters.

Reduced rates for a set period (30 days or less) offered in an introductory letter will get some faster responses but caution is advised. The offer should not be sensationalized (i.e., "If you don't submit your documents before ---- you will miss out on the huge ten percent discount that will never be offered again!"); nor should the offer be worded in a way that could be perceived as coercion.

(I.E., "Submit before ---- and get your ten percent discount as well as fast turn around. After ----, we may not keep you on our mailing list for such services.").

The offer should be plainly stated without such tactics. Example: "A ten percent discount is available for new clients who use our services within 30 days of receiving this letter."

As stated earlier in this book, letterhead paper is not absolutely necessary when you begin your business. By the time you begin direct mail (intro letters) advertising, using letterhead stationery would appear more professional. In any case, always ensure your letters are neat, professional and clean of any smudges or other marks. Signing your letters in a light blue ink gives a personal touch too. Some of the largest mail order businesses also believe

that a typed or handwritten post script
(P. S.)with a final urge for action pays
off for sales letters.

Clients picked up through letter writing are good word-of-mouth advertising
for your business also, because they are
in positions of influence and exposure
to many others who would likewise need
your services.

PAID ADVERTISING

CLASSIFIED ADS

Classified ads will range from a low of
about two dollars per line for local
newspaper and "Penny Saver"/"Shopper"
ads to as high as six dollars per word
or more for magazines.

It is therefore very important that you
choose the right words and target the
right audience for these ads because
you could be wasting a lot of money. As
a rule most "free" or "throw away" newspapers are a waste of advertising dollars when compared to newspapers that
are sold. A large percentage of those
who receive the free publications throw
them away without opening them.

Most newspapers and magazines have
their classifieds divided into specific
sections or subsections, so you need to

review the classifieds of your target
publications first to determine the section you want your ad to appear in.

Your community library will have local
and major national newspapers and
several magazines. If you want to try
the free newspapers, "Penny Savers" or
"Shoppers" can normally be found outside stores in your town or community.

Initial advertising should be limited
to those newspapers in your local community. This gives you a chance to test
your ad for drawing ability (getting
responses) and the feedback is quick
(one to five days). It also keeps your
costs low and risks of losing large
amounts of money are reduced.

You should run the ad at least two con-
secutive times but not more than three.
This gives your ad a fair chance to
prove its drawing ability and does not
lock in a poor, nonproducing ad for a
longer period.

If you advertise in two or more publications, use a KEY to identify which ad
drew the response. You key your ad by
including "Dept," "Suite," or "Drawer"
in your address (right after your
street number or box number) with something that identifies the publication.

For example, if your local newspaper is
called the Pine Tree Flyer, your key
could be Dept-PTF, Suite-PTF, or Drawer-
PTF (i.e., ABC Typing Service, 22 Maple
Street Suite-PTF, Anywhere, USA).

As responses are received, you should
keep good records of which ad and publications are providing the best draws.
This information will then help you decide which publication to continue advertising in, and which ones you should
drop.

A few words on DISPLAY ADS. These ads
are more costly than classified ads and
range in price from $150-$60,000 for a
one-time shot! It is NOT advisable to
use a display ad until your business
has been well established and you see a
clearly defined need to have one.

The advantage of display advertising is
more space is available to describe
your services or to communicate other
information about your business.

Writing

Classified Ads

LOCAL NEWSPAPERS AND PUBLICATIONS

As stated earlier, classifieds cost one to six dollars per word or line for a one time insertion, so you need to limit the number of words and still get the message across. We will discuss magazine ads in a moment, but let's talk about ads in your local newspaper first.

If someone knowledgeable about your typing business will be at home most of the time or you have a telephone answering machine, use your phone number in the local ad rather than an address. This will save several words you will not have to pay for. Some publications have a minimum (such as ten words) and leaving out the address will give you more words to describe your offer.

Chapter Nine/Writing Classified Ads

If you do decide to use only your telephone number, ensure you have a note pad next to your telephone to write down the caller's name, services inquiring about, their address/phone number, and what publication they saw your ad in.

Again, keeping good track of the ad drawing power is essential to making later decisions about advertising in publications.

Getting the person's name, address and phone number is important also.

Your ad interested them enough to call you, and if they decide not to use your services after discussing it with you on the phone, that does not mean they will not be a future client.

When you ask for their name and address, politely state it is for keeping them informed of the range of services that you offer or to notify them of any discount specials. And use it exactly for that purpose. Many times when discussing your business over the phone, important advantages you offer can be skimmed over or forgotten by your prospective client.

A nice letter to them listing your many services and rates and thanking them for their telephone inquiry could very well result in gaining another client.

Chapter Nine/Writing Classified Ads

So what should your classified ad say? The following is only an example and should not be construed as the best approach. It is provided here to il- lustrate use of brevity in your ads while getting your message across:

PROFESSIONAL TYPING AT AFFORDABLE RATES. NEAT, CLEAN, ERROR-FREE. FAST TURN AROUND. CALL 555-1212.

The example has 14 words, counting the phone number. It does not contain the name of your business nor your address, which would take another six to ten words. Keep in mind this is only an option to save advertising costs.

If you do not feel comfortable with or otherwise object to conducting your business over the phone, use your ad- dress in the ad.

You would not want to use a "telephone contact" ad in a national magazine, how- ever. Few prospective clients would opt to pay long distance telephone charges just to inquire about your rates and services when a postage stamp would bring the same information.

Likewise, your business can not afford to accept collect calls from prospec- tive clients. This does not mean you

would not want your business phone number in a national ad. It does mean that
you don't want the phone number as the
only means of contact.

MAGAZINE ADS

Magazine ads are much more expensive
than local newspapers, "Shoppers and
Penny Savers," so you have to ensure
you target the right magazine. For example, if you want to type manuscripts,
you would choose WRITER'S DIGEST rather
than POPULAR MECHANICS.

Choose the service you want to advertise, then select the BEST magazine to
reach your prospective clients.

When advertising in magazines, use abbreviations when practical. This is important when the target publication
charges by line rather than by word; it
allows you to get more information to
your prospective client at a cheaper
price. Naturally, your abbreviations
must be understood or your advertisement will not be effective.

For example, in most magazines that
serve writers, there are several common
abbreviations that you can use and be
confident that your message is getting

across.   The   following   abbreviations
are examples:

SASE = Self Addressed Stamped Envelope

DS = Double Spaced

W/CC = With Carbon Copy

PUB = Published

WP = Word Processing or Word Processor

SPL-CHK = Spell Check

PUNC = Punctuation

CORR = Corrections

CC = Carbon Copy

PG = Page

+POST = Plus Postage (Client pays
        postage)

HNDWRTN = Handwritten

GUAR = Guaranteed

PROF = Professional

INC = Includes or Included

GRAM = Grammar or Grammatical

LEG = Legible

STD = Standard

MBR = Member

STOR = Storage

MS = Manuscript

PC = Personal Computer

ROUGHS = Rough Drafts, unformatted

ADDTL = Additional

PPD = Postage Paid (You pay postage)

TECH = Technical

BK = Book

PRNTR = Printer

EXP = Experience

AVAIL = Available

DOCS = Documents

MNR = Minor

LQ = Letter Quality

EQPT = Equipment

YRS = Years

CONF = Confidential

TRANS = Transcriptions

SAT = Satisfaction

INT'L = International

CLNTS = Clients

ORIG = Original

SVCS = Services

FM = From

RPTS = Reports

DISSER = Dissertations

TRN = Turn Around

MOS = Months

CASS = Cassettes

EXT CPY = Extra Copy

ACCUR = Accurate

JUST MAR = Justified Margins

NLQ = Near Letter Quality

Chapter Nine/Writing Classified Ads

IBM SEL = IBM Selectric Typewriter

20#/25% = Twenty pound, twenty-five
percent cotton paper

While you would not use all of these
abbreviations in one ad, the above list
gives you the flexibility to say a lot
in just a few lines.

For example, if you advertise in a magazine that requires a set rate with a
minimum number of lines -- say ninety
dollars for six lines -- you would use
these abbreviations to say the most you
can within the six lines.

The first three lines would be your address and phone number; the last three
lines would be your offer to clients.
Your ad might look something like this:

A & B Typing Service
3434 Horatio Ave, Anywhere, US 99999
Phone: 555/555-1212
$1.25 DS PG PPD. LQ PRNTR. INC SPL-
CHK,MNR PUNC/GRM CORR. MS, ROUGHS, LEG
HNDWRTN, CASS OK. ORIG + CC, SAT GUAR.

As you can see from the example, using
abbreviations allows you to give a considerable amount of information in the
lines of advertising. If you had not

used abbreviations, your ad would have taken up several additional lines.

At the average cost of fifteen dollars per line, that would have cost you much more.

The appendix lists the addresses of several writer's publications that you can obtain "rate cards" from. These are cards or brochures that give price lists for advertising and shows magazine circulation as well as ad cutoff dates for insertion. These magazines are high quality publications and you will pay premium prices to advertise in them, but responses you receive from prospective clients will be professional and sincere rather than curiosity seekers.

If you decide to advertise in these publications, some of them will ask for an example of your typing and will tell you the format for the example.

TELEPHONE YELLOW PAGES ADVERTISING

This type of advertising is valuable after you are well established and have acquired a business phone. The cost is dependent upon whether you use a display ad or merely list the name of your business, street address and phone number.

You should place your ad under "Secretarial Services," "Typing," or "Printing," depending on how your local phone book is organized.

We talked about naming your business, license and taxes in Chapter Four, but if you advertise in the Yellow Pages the name you choose for your business will have an effect on the response you get from that type of advertising.

Yellow Page advertising is alphabetical within alphabetical categories. The natural tendency of Yellow Page users is to turn to the category and start looking at the first ads that appear, especially if they are in a hurry.

If, for example, your business is named AAA Typing Service, your ad will be one of the first ones read. Conversely, if your business is called Zebra Typing Service, it will be one of the last under that category and may never be read! Just something to keep in mind if you are considering Yellow Page advertising.

Regardless of the type of advertising you decide to use, you will have to write business letters to get things done. And that is where the next chapter will help you.

CHAPTER TEN

Your

Business Letters

WRITTEN COMMUNICATIONS

Business letters are an important part of any business. They are required to do things that cannot be done over the telephone or face-to-face.

How your letters are written says something about you to the receiver. Many decisions are made based on written communications and are driven by the perceptions of the person responsible for taking actions; the person who receives the letter.

If your letter is poorly written, contains grammatical and spelling errors, or does not say anything, the receiver of the correspondence will have little confidence in what you have to say.

You will be writing introductory sales

letters, credit letters, thank you letters, and collection letters. How you write these will determine whether they achieve their intended purpose.

Not everyone is familiar with writing letters of this type. Several books on the subject have been written and sold because the need is so crucial and the level of experience in writing good correspondence is small.

A letter should state the purpose of the correspondence. Active voice should be used rather than passive. The letter should be short but include all the necessary information. Long, rambling letters may get thrown away because the reader loses interest or because they do not have the time to separate the "purpose" from the "clutter."

If words are misspelled or the grammar is bad, the first impression a reader has is that the writer is illiterate. The chance that they will send typing to the correspondent is poor.

You can read "do's" and "don'ts" about letters, but the best lesson is through the use of examples. This chapter will give sample business letters you will need. While they may not be the exact words you want to use in your correspon- dence, they will give you an idea of how the letters should be written. You may decide to use them verbatim, changing only the information that is peculiar to your needs.

INTRODUCTORY SALES LETTERS.

The purpose of sales letters is to let prospective clients know you are in business and to get them as clients. The letter should appeal to their needs and your ability to satisfy them.

This may be your one chance to get them as a client, so you need to create your best professional impression. Your letter needs to convey stability, professional competence, sincerity and a customer-oriented service. A big order, but easily done when the right words are used.

Authorities say that one of the biggest expenses for a business is letter writing. To create a letter takes time, and time is money. The average business letter takes four to seven hours to create and polish, a big expense when considering the alternatives those hours could be used for.

The following letters are examples for your use. They can be modified to suit your needs or used as a point of reference for your own style.

For most small businesses, hiring a
secretary as a regular employee can be
a significant financial burden on
their operating budget. Inflation,
federal and state government regula-
tions, office equipment, and the high
turnover rate for typist and secretarial employees have forced many small
businesses into uncomfortable situations.

Funds to reinvest into the growth of
their business are reduced consider-
ably; finding a professional typist or
secretary at the salary they can afford is difficult; and when the secretary is not available because they
have moved on to work for someone
else, critical correspondence piles up
while the business owner scrambles to
try and find a replacement typist.

Our typing service can help you. We
provide professional typing at an affordable rate. You only pay for the
actual time spent typing and your overhead is reduced. The enclosed rate
sheet describes our services and exam-
ines the best arrangement for small
businesses that need outside secretarial services.

Our business has a continuing commit-
ment to providing quality professional

typing for our customers. Please write or call so we can discuss your needs. We look forward to hearing from you.

Sincerely,

_____

Everyone's talking about quality ... reading stories and seeing telecasts about economy ... but let us examine just how these two words become real when you use our typing services.

... They are real because our typing is professional, error-free workman-ship based on experience and under-standing of today's business communi-cation needs. We can satisfy your typing needs at half the cost you would pay for a permanent typist or secretarial employee.

That's why many small businesses are turning to outside secretarial help... why your type of business will have more capital to reinvest ... why secre-tarial services have the reputations of providing the best for less.

Right NOW we are accepting new clients for the many services we offer. The enclosed rate sheet gives our current prices and lists the many advantages of using our secretarial help. Won't you write or call us and tell us your needs?

Sincerely,

_____

Why do thousands use it? Because a secretarial service is not just a typing agency, but a time-saving method to get your documents typed into a professional, quality product.

Our staff has the experience you need. We provide quick turn around, type your product in whatever format you want and at an affordable rate.

Like everyone, your time is valuable. You give your typing needs to us, and it's done. No more missed opportunities to do more important things.

Our enclosed rate sheet provides all the information you need to review the advantages we offer. Act NOW, and you will receive a 10 percent discount on your first submission. We look forward to hearing from you.

Sincerely,
* * * * * * * * * * * * * * *

Sometimes you will receive letters from prospective clients asking for credit. Here, you must be very careful.

A good rule of thumb is to not grant credit to individuals using your services for the first time. If they have used your services several times on a cash basis, you have a better idea of whether the person is credit worthy.

Did the person pay by cash or check before? Were any of the checks returned for nonpayment? Has the client complained about your quality or cost? If they paid cash before, why are they asking for credit now? Be curious. It is better to deny credit than it is to spend your valuable time and efforts for free.

Many businesses work on a credit basis, paying their bills once a month. They usually establish lines of credit, a set amount of open-ended credit that they are allowed to use.

It will be a judgement call on your part, but you can reduce the risk by a little research.

Write or call your local Better Business Bureau. Give them the name of the business and inquire about financial complaints or problems they may be aware of. Ask for references from the

business client that you can check out.
If you know of other secretarial services in your community, call them and
inquire if they have conducted business
with your prospective client. You can
never be too careful. Be firm in your
efforts; you are in business to make a
profit, not provide charitable secretarial services.

In situations where you cannot get information on the credit worthiness of a
business, do their first job on a cash
basis or combination cash/credit arrangement and ask that they provide you
additional credit references you can
use to do future jobs on credit.

If the client's intentions are honor-
able, they will agree to these arrangements without any problems. If they pro-
test and seem indignant, you are better
off without their business.

The following letters are examples that
can be used to reply to requests for
credit. They can be modified to give
information about your credit policy,
grant credit, or refuse credit.

We are pleased to have your contract
to use our typing services for your

daily typing requirements.

To assist us in setting up arrangements to service your needs, will you please send us a current financial statement and the names of three businesses that now deal with you on a credit basis.

We can easily handle the volume of typing you estimate and provide the finished products to you well within your specified time limits. We look forward to the opportunity of serving your needs.

Sincerely,

_____

(Letter to business references given by prospective client)

We have received a first-time contract application from a firm whom we believe you are now doing business; the Doorway Construction Company of Naples, Florida.

In their application for establishing a line of credit, the Doorway Company submitted the name of your business as a reference.

So that we may accept the contract and begin servicing their secretarial needs promptly, we respectfully ask for your cooperation in giving information on the Doorway Company. In particular, we would like to know how long you have conducted business with their company, what credit limit you have placed on their account, how promptly terms are satisfied, and what amount is currently outstanding.

Thank you for your help. We hope to have the opportunity some day to assist you in a like manner.

Sincerely,

_____

We have reviewed your recent inquiry about using our services on a credit basis.

Before establishing credit, we always try to get information that will justify giving the credit requested. However, we do not have enough information in your case to grant the credit you asked for. Maybe future situations will change and we can service your needs on credit.

Meanwhile, we hope you will take

advantage of our fast, professional service and affordable rates.

Sincerely,

_____

You may occasionally have credit customers who have passed the due date without paying you. When this happens, you
will need to write a collection letter.

When writing collection letters, you
should consider the circumstances sur-
rounding their failure to pay.

Because credit ratings are so important
to individuals and businesses alike,
you need to be sensitive to the words
you use. Your approach to the problem
needs to be tactful and professional.
Try to use a tone that will not cause
anger, resentment, irritation, or indif-
ference.

_____

Just a reminder that your account is
past due in the amount of $45.56 and
that prompt payment would be in keeping with your past good record.
Thanks.

Sincerely,

_____

Review of your account reveals there still remains a small overdue balance of $30.75. Prompt payment will be appreciated.

Thank you.

Sincerely,

This is sent as a friendly reminder of your past due account of $50.78 that we believe you have overlooked.

We are sure you intended to pay as promptly as you have in the past.

If your payment has already been sent, please disregard this letter.

Thank you.

Sincerely,

Your account, with a past-due balance of $40.34, has just been placed in our "overdue file." Therefore, it is time to remind you that you owe us some money. If you have already remitted the balance due, please accept our thanks.

Sincerely,

Sometimes your initial collection letters go unanswered. Whatever the reason, you will need to send follow-up letters. If you do not follow up, you may not get paid.

Your follow-up letters should be spaced about two to three weeks apart, depending on the payment arrangements you set up for your client. Here are some examples of follow-up letters.

April 1 we wrote you about your past due balance in the amount of $35.00. We have not heard from you.

Perhaps there is a reason why you have not sent payment; we would appreciate you writing to let us know. Otherwise, we assume your past due account was an oversight and that you will mail your payment within the next few days.

Sincerely,

You probably have a reason you have not answered our letter about your past-due account of $60.00. Maybe you did not get our statement, your check was mailed to the wrong address, or our accounts receivable was never posted. Whatever the reason, we want to hear from you.

You need to answer our letter. We want to be paid what we earned and want you to feel free to use our secretarial services again.

By paying your past-due account, you will allow us to continue serving your typing needs. That will be the best course of action for your business -- and ours.

We expect to hear from you soon.

Cordially,

If a second letter gets no response, then you must assume the client intends to slow pay or not to pay at all. You are probably better off without their business and the hassle of trying to get your money every time you type for them. In that case, you need to become firm in your demand for payment.

———————————

This is the fourth letter we have sent you about your past-due account of $55.00. It was due more than three months ago.

Your line of credit was opened based on the agreement that we would provide you with fast, professional secretarial services and that you would make payment according to our schedule. We have lived up to our part of the arrangement. You should live up to yours.

We would Appreciate receiving your payment of $55.00 immediately.

Cordially,

———————————

Your credit standing is valuable. We do not believe you would like to see it damaged because you failed to pay your past-due account of $50.00; the payment was due three months ago.

Your use of our continued secretarial services is at stake and so is your ability to get credit from others.

We believe you Know the seriousness of this situation. You must protect your credit record by taking the morally correct actions of paying your debts.

We expect your check for full payment immediately.

Cordially,

_____

Your credit in the amount of $75.00 is now so far past due that immediate payment is the only measure that will prevent us from taking legal action.

We have used up our patience to get you to pay your just debts. We have had no cooperation whatsoever from you.

Taking legal action for collection and reporting your bad credit standing is our next move.

If we do not receive your payment by April 21, we will take the actions described above.

Cordially,

_____

If your final ultimatum letters do not result in receipt of payment, you have several options.

You can turn collection of the debt over to a collection agency or a lawyer. The charge is usually one third (1/3) of the overdue amount.

You can contact the Better Business Bureau and/or local trade associations your client belongs to and inform them of the situation. Sometimes they will attempt to contact the delinquent creditor on your behalf. More often, they will record the derogatory information and provide it to any future inquirers about the credit worthiness of the client.

You can contact your state Attorney General for help. You can also provide a credit report to national credit bureaus.

Finally, you can decide to do nothing and write off the bad credit as noncollectable. If the amount owed is small, this may be the most hassle-free course of action.

Just be sure your records reflect the noncredit worthiness of the business or individual so that you do not extend future credit.

THANK YOU LETTERS.

These types of letters are an important part of your good will with clients. A thank you, whether a short, handwritten note or a typed letter, is always appreciated. It could also result in repeat business or word-of-mouth referrals to new clients. It never hurts to take the time to say thanks.

We are pleased to send you the completed typing of your short story, "My Life on the Farm." Your check in the amount of $38.00 was correct, and appreciated.

Thank you for using our typing service. It's nice customers like you that make our business so rewarding.

We look forward to serving your typing needs again.

Very truly yours,

Since we began servicing your secretarial needs over two months ago, we have been quite pleased with your absolute professionalism and friendly patronage.

We just want to say "thank you" for being so great a client!

It is clients like you that make our daily business world so rewarding. Your prompt payment, clear instructions, and expressions of satisfaction with our services are greatly appreciated.

We extend our sincere thanks to you for choosing our organization to service your typing and secretarial needs.

We look forward to a long and professional relationship with one of the most outstanding clients we have ever conducted business!

Very truly yours,

* * * * * * * * * * * * * * *

Afterword

CONDUCTING BUSINESS

SUCCESS

Now that you have carefully read the preceding chapters, you should be prepared to start your home typing business with complete confidence in your ability to succeed.

Before closing this last chapter, there are a few thoughts to be left with you about your business.

"Secretary" is almost always used synonymously with typing, and the key part of the word "Secretary" is SECRET. Any thing you type for clients must be done in a confidential manner and should never be discussed in conversation with anyone except your client.

Integrity is priceless to the success or failure of your business, and should be high in the priority scheme of how you conduct your business.

Being considerate -- but firm -- always gains respect from everyone, especially your clients. The old adage "Do unto others ... " is the best advice one could heed.

You will succeed in your business because you have the initiative to establish an income-earning venture for your valuable time. You may even find, as others have, that expanding your business to a full time profession is the way you want to go.

We are always happy to hear from those who have used this book to start their business and would like to hear from you too. If you have any suggestions for improving on the content, we would be glad to have your feedback. Comments can be mailed to:

Supertext Publishing
213-A 4th Street, Suite 201
Honolulu, HI 96818-4937

We wish you the greatest success in your endeavors.

Appendices

GENERAL FORMATS FOR MANUSCRIPT TYPING

PAPER: 8.5" X 11.5", 20 pound/25 percent cotton fiber. Type on one side only.

RIBBON: Clean, clear, black.

TYPE SIZE: 10 pitch Pica, if available; 12 pitch Elite OK.

HEADER: This is information typed at the top of a page (flush with the left-hand margin) that gives short title and last name of author. Example: If the title of the manuscript was "The Complete Typing Business Guide," by Frank Chisenhall, "Typing Business Guide/Chisenhall" would be the header on the Book Title page. For each chapter afterwards, The chapter and last name of author would be used. Example: Chapter One/Chisenhall. Headers are typed eight to nine (8-9) lines from the top of the page (1 1/4" to 1 1/2" from top of page). Type headers on each page of the manuscript.

MARGINS: 1 1/4" to 1 1/2" all around (top, bottom, sides).

TEXT: Start six (6) lines (1-inch) down from headers.

PAGE NUMBERS: Top right-hand corner on same line as Header. DO NOT NUMBER TITLE PAGES. The Title pages count in the total number of pages, but are not numbered.

SPACING: Always double-space, with the following exceptions:

1. Client requests different spacing.

2. Single-space quotations that are more than three typewritten lines.

3. Single-space bibliographies.

4. Single-space footnotes.

5. Triple-space before and after quotations that are separated from text bv indentations.

6. Quadruple-space between each title and the text that follows for:

 a. Biographies.

 b. Notes.

 c. References.

 d. Appendices and indexes.

 e. Introductions.

 f. Bibliographies.

g. Acknowledgments.

7. Single-space headings or titles that require two or more typewritten lines.

8. Triple-space between titles and subtitles.

9. Always begin new chapter or other major division of a manuscript on a new page.

10. Center and capitalize all headings.

11. Pages other than manuscript text are not numbered; i. e., Title page, Preface, Contents page, etc.

The following section will give examples of:

1. Nonfiction manuscripts.

2. Fiction manuscripts.

3. Articles.

4. Short stories.

The examples will include a title page, chapter page, and first page of text.

NONFICTION Manuscript Format

TITLE Page:

(Line 8 or 9) Client's Name & Address, flush with left margin. Word count is on same line, flush with right margin.

Manuscript Title (line 20 or 21), (Each word capitalized -- upper/lowercase -- centered approximately 20-21 lines from top of page).

(lower right-hand corner, within margins) Agent's Name & Address, if Requested.

 ALWAYS maintain 1 1/4" to 1 1/2" Margins!

NONFICTION Chapter heading page:

(line 8 or 9) Header: Typing Bus/Doe, flush with left margin. Page # on same line, flush with right margin.

(line 15) Chapter One (Flush with left margin)

(line 18) Getting Started (chapter subject, Flush with left margin) (line 25) indent and begin typing double-spaced text.

<u>NONFICTION Chapter text,</u> second and subsequent pages.

(line 8 or 9) Header: Chapter One/Doe, flush left margin. Page # on same line, flush right margin.

(line 15 or 16) Begin text. If new paragraph, indent.

Maintain 1 1/4" to 1 1/2" all around margins.

<u>FICTION Manuscript Format</u>

TITLE Page:

(line 8 or 9) Client's Name & Address (flush left-hand margin. same line, flush right-hand margin, type wordage (Number of words in the manuscript).

MANUSCRIPT TITLE (line 18, center, all Caps!)

A Novel By (line 21, upper/lowercase)

Appendices/Standard Typing Formats

John Doe (Author's name, line 24, upper/lowercase)

(lower right-hand corner) Agent's name & Address, if requested. If this address used, leave off client's address.

ALWAYS maintain 1 1/4" to 1 1/2" Margins.

FICTION Chapter heading page:

(line 8 or 9) Header: THE MIDWEEK BUST (Title of Book, All Caps). Header flush with left margin. Same line, page # flush with right margin.

(line 22) CHAPTER One--GETTING CAUGHT (All Caps, centered.)

(line 29) Indent; double-spaced text begins.

_____

FICTION Chapter text, second and subsequent pages.

(line 8 or 9) Header: THE MIDWEEK BUST--Chapter II. Flush left-hand margin. Page #, flush right margin.

(line 15) Text begins, double-spaced, indented if new paragraph.

Maintain 1 1/4" to 1 1/2" all around margins.

* * * * * * * * * * * * * * * * *

Magazine & Newspaper ARTICLE Formats

TITLE Page:

(line 8 or 9) Type of "rights" offered; i.e., First Serial Rights Only. Under this, indicate word count. (All this information is typed flush with right-hand margin).

(line 32) ARTICLE TITLE (All Caps, centered)

(line 35) "by" (lowercase, centered)

(line 37) JOHN DOE (Author's name, All Caps, centered)

(Flush, bottom left-hand margin) Address. Do not include name again unless pen name is reflected as Article author.   Last line of address should maintain margin requirement (1 1/4" to 1 1/2" from bottom).

ARTICLE First Page Format:

(line 8 or 9) Author's name, address, and phone # flush with left margin. "Rights" offered & word count are same line (Flush with right margin). NO PAGE NUMBER!

110

Appendices/Standard Typing Formats

(line 23) ARTICLE TITLE (All Caps, centered)

(line 26) Author's Name (Example: by John Doe), Upper and lowercase, centered.

(line 31) Begin text. Indent, double-space.

ARTICLE Second and subsequent pages Format:

(line 8 or 9) Header: last name of author and short title description: i. e. , Doe/Typing. Header is flush left margin and page # is flush right-hand margin, same line as header.

(line 15) Begin text. Double-space and indent if starting a new paragraph.

ALWAYS Maintain the required 1 1/4" or 1 1/2" margins all around.

SHORT STORY First Page Format:

(line 8 or 9) Author's name, address and phone #, flush with left margin. "Rights" offered and word count, flush with right margin. NO PAGE NUMBER!

111

(line 23) SHORT STORY TITLE (All caps, centered)

(line 26) "by" (lowercase, centered)

(line 29) AUTHOR'S NAME (All caps, centered)

(line 34) Begin story. Indent, double-space.

SHORT STORY Second and subsequent pages:

(line 8) Last name of author (Upper/lowercase, Flush left margin. PAGE NUMBER is also on line #8, flush with right-hand margin.

(line 15) Begin text. Indent if starting new paragraph, double-space.

ALWAYS Maintain 1 1/4" to 1 1/2" all around margin.

RESUME FORMATS

CHRONOLOGICAL RESUME (single-spaced):

(line 8) Client's name, address, home & business phone, flush left margin.

Birth date on same line, flush right margin.

NOTE: Line 9-13 information will all be typed flush right margin.

(line 9) Height: (feet/inches)

(line 10) Weight: (pounds)

(line 11) Marital status

(line 12) Number of children,

(line 13) Willingness to relocate

(line 18) Work Experience (Type this header flush with left margin).

(line 21) Date (last job held date to present. Example: 1982-Present). Type flush with left margin. JOB TITLE (all caps, centered) with name and address of employer typed beneath (centered, Upper/lowercase) on same line.

(line 28) begin description of job. Indent entire paragraph. Usually 12-15 line paragraph.

Double-space between each chronological insertion. Maintain 1 1/4" to 1 1/2" margins all around.

_____

FUNCTIONAL RESUME FORMAT (single-
spaced):

(line 8) Client's name & address, flush
left margin. Same line, flush right
margin, type Home phone #.

(line 9) Office Phone: (flush, right
margin).

(line 16) Job Objective:
(Upper/lowercase, flush left margin.
Short one-sentence objective statement
about job person is seeking.

(line 21) Work History
(Upper/lowercase, flush left margin).

(line 24) Last Job Title held
(Upper/lowercase, flush left margin).

(line 27) Begin description of last job
held.   Usually 12-15 line paragraph,
entire paragraph indented.   End of paragraph, skip one line, give employer's
name and address.   Skip one line again,
and give inclusive dates.

Skip three lines between each additional chronological insertion.   Maintain 1
1/4" to 1 1/2" margin all around.

This appendix contains the addresses of Writing and Journalism publications. The following abbreviations apply:

TEL = Telephone

CIR = Circulation count

FREQ = Frequency that publication is published.

If you wish to advertise your home typing services in any of these publications, address your requests for Rate Cards to the Classified Advertising Department.

WRITER'S DIGEST, F & W Publications, 9933 Alliance Road, Cincinnati, OH 45242. TEL: 513-984-0717. CIR: 225,000. FREQ: Monthly.

WRITER, INC., 120 Boylston Street, Boston, MA 02116. TEL: 617-423-3157. CIR: 57,418. FREQ: Monthly

BOOKLIST, American Library Association, 50 East Huron Street, Chicago, IL 60611. TEL: 312-944-6780. CIR: 37,000. FREQ: 22 per year

WASHINGTON JOURNALISM REVIEW,
Associates, Inc., 2233 Wisconsin
Avenue, Washington, DC 20007. CIR:
32,000. FREQ: Monthly

WESTERN PUBLISHER, INC., Box 591012,
Golden Gate Station, San Francisco, CA
94159. TEL: 415-221-1964. CIR: 10,000.
FREQ: Monthly

WRITERS GUILD OF AMERICA, WEST, 8955
Beverly Blvd, Los Angeles, CA 90048.
TEL: 213-550-1000. CIR: 7,000. FREQ:
Monthly

CHOICE (MIDDLETOWN), Association of
College and Research Libraries, 100
Riverview Center, Middletown, CT 06457.
TEL: 203-347-6933. CIR: 5,300. FREQ:
Monthly

WRITERS CONNECTION, 1601 Saratoga,
Sunnyvale Road, Suite 180, Cupertino, CA
95014. TEL: 408-973-0227. CIR: 3,000.
FREQ: Monthly

SCHOOL PRESS REVIEW, Columbia
University, Box 11, Central Mail Room,
New York, NY 10027-6969. TEL: 212-280-
3311

WORLD LITERATURE TODAY, University of
Oklahoma Press, 110 monnet Hall,
University of Oklahoma, Norman, OK
73019. TEL: 405-325-4531. CIR: 2,500.
FREQ: Quarterly

WRITER'S JOURNAL, Inkling Publications.
Inc, Box 65-798, St Paul, MN 55165-0798.
TEL: 612-221-0326. CIR: 1,600. FREQ: Bi-
Monthly

SOUTHEASTERNER (Newspaper), University
of Kentucky, Southeast Community
College, Cumberland, KY 40823. TEL: 606-
589-2145. CIR: 1,500. FREQ: Monthly
(Sep-May)

WAYSTATION FOR THE SF WRITER, Unique
Graphics, 1025 55th St, Oakland, CA
94608. TEL: 415-655-3024. CIR: 1,433.
FREQ: Quarterly

WRITER'S GAZETTE, Trouvere Company, Rt 2,
Box 290, Eclectic, AL 36024. CIR:
1,200. FREQ: Quarterly

TPA MESSENGER (Tabloid format), Texas
Press Association, 718 W. 5th St.,
Austin, TX 78701. TEL: 512-477-6755.
CIR: 1,015. FREQ: Monthly

WRITING INSTRUCTOR, Univ. of Southern
California, Freshman Writing Program, Los
Angeles, CA 90089-0062. CIR: 950. FREQ:
Quarterly

IF you have a word processor or computer with word processing capabilities, can store documents on diskette,
and have a good letter quality printer,
below are some possible publications
for advertising. It would not hurt to
send copies of your news releases to
these people also.

COSMEP, P. O. Box 703, San
Francisco, CA 94101.

National Federation of Press
Women, Box 99, Blue Springs, MO
64015.

The National Writers Club, 1450
South Havana, Suite 620, Aurora, CO
80012.

Women in Communications, Inc.,
Box 9561, Austin, TX 78766.

Publishers Weekly, 249 West 17th
Street, New York, NY 10011

Bibliography

ADDITIONAL SOURCES OF INFORMATION

This compilation represents various
sources available for additional information that may be useful in the conduct and success of your typing business. Publisher addresses not listed
may be found in Books In Print, a
reference work that can be reviewed in
your community library.

FORMAT REFERENCES.

The Writer's Digest Guide To Manuscript Formats, by Dian Dincin
Buchman and Seli Groves. Discusses how
to prepare/present book manuscripts,
magazine articles, short stories, cover
letters, proposals, queries, fillers,
poems, plays, movies, audio-visual,
television scripts, photos, and illus-
trations. A must guide for typists who
service authors. Published by Writer's
Digest Books, 1507 Dana Avenue, Cincinnati, OH, 45207.

MLA Handbook, by Modern Language

Association of America. Provides format
guidance for writers of research
papers, theses, and dissertations.
Covers basic English mechanics as well
as general formats. Published by the
Modern Language Association of America,
New York.

Chicago Manual of Style, by University of Chicago Press. Style guide
used by typists, publishers, editors,
and writers. Covers the basics of printing, typesetting, grammar and style.
Published by the University of Chicago
Press.

A Practical Style Guide For Authors
and Editors, by Margaret Nicholson.
Presents general format information.
Published by Holt, Rinehart, and
Winston.

COMPUTER AND WORD PROCESSING INFORMATION

Word Processing and Information Processing, by Dan Poynter. A basic manual on What they are and How to buy. A
comprehensive guide written in easy-to-
understand language. Published by Para
Publishing, P. O. Box 4232, Santa Barbara, CA, 93140-4232.

Bibliography/Recommended Reading

Computer Selection Guide, by Dan
Poynter.   Choosing the right Hardware
and Software: Business, Professional,
Personal. Published by Para Publishing,
P. O. Box 4232, Santa Barbara, CA, 93140-
4232.

How To Buy A Personal Computer,
by U. S. Office of Consumer Affairs.
Step-by-step guide to selecting a computer, floppy disks, and printer. See
BUSINESS INFORMATION section for how to
order.

_____

LETTER WRITING INFORMATION

Better Letters, by Jan Venolia.
A hand-book of business and personal
correspondence.   Published by Ten Speed
Press, P. O. Box 7123, Berkeley, CA,
94707.

Complete Secretary's Handbook, by
Lillian Doris and Bessie May Miller.
Published by Prentice-Hall, Inc.

Revising Business Prose, by
Richard Lanham.   Published by Charles
Scribner's Sons.

Business Writing, by J. Harold
Janis and Howard R. Dressner. Published
by Barnes and Noble Books, a division
of Harper and Row, Publishers.

Bibliography/Recommended Reading

BUSINESS INFORMATION

<u>Earn Money At Home,</u> by Peter
Davidson.   Published by McGraw-Hill.

<u>Homebased Businesses,</u> edited by
Beverly N. Feldman.   Published by Till
Press.

<u>How To Start a Profitable Typing
Service at Home,</u> by Nicki Montaperto
(1981).   Published by Barnes and Noble.

<u>Invest In Yourself: A Woman's Guide
to Starting Her Own Business,</u> by Peg
Moran.   Published by Doubleday.

FEDERAL INFORMATION SOURCES. Many helpful books can be ordered from the federal government. For a free Consumer Information Catalog listing these, write
to: R. Woods, Consumer Information
Center-L, P. O. Box 100, Pueblo, CO,
81002.

Write to the U. S. Small Business Administration, P. O. Box 15434, Fort Worth,
TX, 76119, to obtain a <u>Directory of
Business Development Publications</u>
order form.   Most of the publications
offered cost one dollar or less and are
well worth ordering.

Index

Index

R

S

T

W

About The Author

Frank Chisenhall has written numerous documents over the past 15 years for various organizations within the military. With a BA from Saint Leo College and an MA from Central Michigan University -- both degrees in business administration and management -- his knowledge in establishing sound business practices has been successfully applied time and again by users of his advice.

Before college, the author had a deep interest in the art of making money at home. He started his first home typing business while in high school with a five-dollar, used Underwood brand typewriter purchased at an auction.

Typing after school and on weekends, he created a real money-maker. His typing resulted in repeat business and new clients from word-of-mouth advertising. For his remaining years in high school, he received a steady income.

The author established a second home typing business after entering the military. The experiences he learned in high school ensured the success of his new venture. His second home business ended when he was assigned to a remote overseas tour.

For the past two years, using his own experiences, college education and in-depth research, the author wrote and prepared The Complete TYPING BUSINESS Guide.

The author observed two trends: that the two-person family income was becoming a real necessity, but was having a severe impact on families with small children; and that a growing shortage of qualified secetaries was creating a need for independent typing businesses. He wrote The Complete TYPING BUSINESS Guide to solve both of these social problems.

The author currently lives with his family in Honolulu, HI and is writing additional "How-To" business books that will be published by SuperText Publishing in the fall of 1990.

ORDER FORM

SuperText Publishing
502 Brantwood Court
Valrico, Fl 33594-2905

Please send me____copies of The
Complete TYPING BUSINESS Guide @
$12.95 each. I understand that I may
return the book(s) for a full refund
if not satisfied.

NAME: _____

ADDRESS: _____

_____ZIP: _____

Shipping Charges:
Book Rate: $1.75 for first book and
75 cents for each additional book.
(Allow three to four weeks for
shipping.)

Send $3 per book for First Class.

****

____Please send FREE information
    on the following additionnal books
    by Frank Chisenhall:

  __ACTION LETTERS FOR SMALL
    BUSINESSES. ($14.95 each)

  __THE COMPLETE GUIDE TO
    TYPING FORMATS. ($16.95 each)

_____

128